I0489974

QuickBooks

Best Way to Learn QuickBooks within a day to optimize bookkeeping!

(QuickBooks, Bookkeeping, QuickBooks Online, QuickBooks 2016, ... Business Taxes, Small Business Accounting)

By:

James Stevens

Published by Shepal Publishing
All Rights Reserved
Copyright 2016, New York

Table of Contents

Introduction

Being organized has amazing benefits as it can save you a lot of time and money, help you achieve success in the least time possible and guarantee happiness. This is the same with an organized business. Business people find it really hard to stay 100% organized and this is one of the reasons why so much time is lost in a business. If you want to achieve better results in your business, staying organized is one sure way to get there.

Bookkeeping is one way through which a business person cannot fail in staying organized. A business has a strong focus on finances that is, what is being received as well as being spent. Financial records in a business matter more than anything else. If they are not well kept, a business can seriously lose money. Bookkeeping can however help you enjoy all the benefits of staying organized and so many more.

QuickBooks have come as a great relief for business people who are always on the go, and are therefore unable to keep up with their business financial records. Bookkeeping should be done on an everyday basis, which is not easy for many business people. With QuickBooks, this can be done much easier and the benefits it comes with are many.

If you are in business, you need to know everything there is in QuickBooks so as to be able to utilize QuickBooks with confidence. You need to learn how to create invoices and sales receipts, and this is something that you can learn in a day through this guide.

Chapter 1:
QuickBooks Basics

QuickBooks is an accounting software that is used by business people who want to keep their business finances accurate and well organized all the time. With QuickBooks, you do not need accounting knowledge; the software does most of the work for you. QuickBooks comes with basic accounting, invoicing and reporting capabilities. Other than that, it will help you handle things like payroll, credit card processing, inventory tracking among others.

Why this is important

It is not easy to keep track of business finances manually and ensure that they are accurate and up to date all the time. After sometime, one can easily get tired and overwhelmed, considering there is still so much to do in an office. That is why many business people prefer to use software to keep everything in order as they attend to other important matters in the business.

Basically, software will help you keep track of the money that the business is receiving and money that you are spending on an everyday basis, to keep track of the money that the business owes others and how much others owe it. Through the software, one can easily know just how well the business is doing at any time of the year. Business people who have been doing all this manually should know how much they are missing out and how much time they are wasting, which can be useful in the business in other ways.

QuickBooks is more than an accounting program. It is a program that will bring out the most creative strategy of your business. It will help you make smart choices that affect every bit of your business fast enough. This is the way business people need to go in order to complete their business tasks in an automated way, which is essential for any business that is growing. As your business grows, the software should be able to handle everything.

QuickBooks helps to manage the following:

- Disbursement tracking

- Data synching

- Record of daily financial dealings

- Automated invoicing of periodic accounts

- Bills and salary payments

Getting started

Once you get your QuickBooks software, the first thing you need to do is to customize it. This is because the program works automatically and customizing it will make it more useful in your business. Personalizing your software will help it serve your most basic needs. This is how you will customize it:

1. The industry type: setting your program to your industry will give you access to some of the best charts that are suitable for your industry. You might choose to use those charts or reject them later for better ones.

2. The business type: this is an important part of the process. Setting this will make your tax preparations

simpler and it will also determine how your charts accounts will be controlled.

3. The invoice type: set your invoices in the way that you want them to appear, for instance in the color, layout and images of your preference. Ensure that you present information in your invoices the way that you feel will be appropriate for your clients.

4. Download preferences: downloads will always be done on your own schedule, therefore change this setting so as to only get downloads when you need them

5. The vending techniques: this will be important because the program will work as per what you are selling, where you are selling it from and also how much you are selling it for. This is the category that will help you to enter and pay your business bills. It will help you control your stock much easier through its different categories like enter bills against and receive inventory.

6. Banking: this is an important function that will help you view your banking activities in a clearer way. It will also help you create and print checks for your customers.

7. Chart of accounts: you need a clean chart of accounts.

8. Customers: this category enables one to generate sales receipts through point of sale creation.

Chapter 2:
Bookkeeping

Bookkeeping entails the recording and organization of financial transactions systematically in a business. Bookkeeping happens on a day to day basis. It is an important thing in any business because it ensures that all financial records in a business are accurate, comprehensive and up to date. Bookkeeping is within the broader scope of accounting and it aims at keeping a good record of information from the accounts in which they are prepared.

In a business, every transaction must be recorded. Every sale and purchase must be put into record as soon as it happens in order to ensure that every detail is in record for effective accountability. There are structures that are usually set in place for bookkeeping, which are referred to as quality controls. These structures are the ones that ensures that everything is recorded in a timely and accurate recording.

Its Importance

Record keeping and bookkeeping are very important for your business. Here are some of the important reasons why every business person needs to take good care of their bookkeeping:

1. To avoid an audit: so many small businesses are audited by an external body because of messy records, and this is something that business people can easily avoid if they keep their business records well. A significant amount of time is spent dealing with external auditors and a lot of money can be spent in the process. To be on the safe side, you should keep all your

business records well and you will not have to deal with an external auditor.

2. To report to investors easily: investors will always want some important information from your business on a regular basis. You need accurate and up to date information that will give then an idea of how your business is doing. Your book of accounts will give you good charts, graphs and a lot of data that you can easily interpret to your investors.

3. To avoid missing important deductions: sometimes it is hard to keep up with important tax deductions especially when your financial records are not in good order. To avoid missing out on such an important detail, you need to keep all your record in order. This way, you can always tell when your tax deductions are legitimate and when they are not.

4. For better financial analysis and management: management of cash flow in a business is very important if you want to follow up on customer's payments on time. This is something that has to be done on time in order to ensure that things are moving smoothly in the business. You do not want to fall out on your supplier's payments as this could delay a lot of things in a business. With such records, you can also do an up to date follow up on financial matters in your business.

5. To save time; bookkeeping on a daily basis helps to save extra time in the long run. With properly kept financial records, you can easily file your tax returns without wasting time looking for important paperwork. You do not need more time to record transactions as you go but

it will cost you a lot of time if you were to do bookkeeping at once.

6. Maintaining a clear picture about your business performance: the health of a business is always determined by how good its financial records are. From the financial record, you can tell if the business is doing well or not, which is something that you need to know every day so as to make the necessary adjustments especially if your business is not performing well. It is impossible to know if you are really making money or not if you do not keep a good record of your business income and expenditure.

Recording transactions in a business

The books of accounts system should be handled on a day to day bass. This is the principle that every business person should take note of. For every transaction, there is a document where it can fit in. Such documents are sale invoice, suppliers invoice, sales receipts, journals, bank payments among others. These documents come with an audit trail for every transaction that you are recording. The audit trail is the one that ensures that all your records are maintained in an accurate manner in the occurrence of an audit.

There is the double entry bookkeeping, which is based on the fact that every transaction has two sides, which affects two types of ledger accounts. There is the debit entry in one account and there is the credit entry into another account. The two accounts have to balance in the end and in case of an error, you can be sure that the recording as not done correctly.

Chapter 3:
QuickBooks Online

Solid accounting is the number one support system in any business and QuickBooks is known as the best accounting system that is suitable for any small business. With the software, you can easily organize your sales through a good track of your expenses, organization of your timesheets, preparing of invoices and sales slips. The software will also help you keep a good track of your tax information. QuickBooks are available as QuickBooks desktop and QuickBooks online and both of them are really good. The choice that you make is mainly determined by the kind of business you are running.

QuickBooks desktop

This program comes with a lot of customized features which many businesses will need. It is good in inventory tracking, budgeting and time tracking. This is the program that will help you determine the area where you are spending so much money in a business in order to cut down on the expenditure to maximize on the income. Many business people use this version of QuickBooks as an investment for the benefits it offers to the business.

QuickBooks online

QuickBooks online is the kind of program that is best suited for a business person that is always on the go therefore he can outsource a bookkeeper or an accountant. This version of QuickBooks comes with one great feature which is the cloud feature. This is the version that will enable a business person to perform customer billing automatically as well as email reports. With this version, you can keep your financial records accurately as well as get enough time to go out there to ensure that your customers are getting the information that they need on time. It is therefore a very flexible program for a business person.

This is the much preferred version for many business people because it gives you access to the basic features of an accountant.

The cost of QuickBooks online is much lower than the QuickBooks desktop. You get to enjoy using it for free for an entire month before you can invest in the program. This is what makes it the best program for those business people that are starting up.

This is what you get from QuickBooks online

1. Automated customer billing instead of doing it manually which can be inaccurate and time consuming.

2. Automated email reports which saves so much time and also provides accurate information for your clients.

3. So many people can use the program at a go.

4. It provides an activity log which enables everyone to track down what they have done so far. You can also see what your employers are doing at any given time.

5. It gives users a simultaneous access to data. You do not need to wait for one to work on a document for you to use it, which costs a business so much time.

The cloud benefits of QuickBooks online

Buying, building and maintaining a functional IT structure is a requirement in business these days but with the increasing prices, small businesses are not able to achieve their desires because of financial limitations. The cloud gives businesses of all kinds and sizes a great alternative in that businesses can now subscribe to shared services online. The benefits of this are so many, for instance you do not have to pay for the services fully since there are several other businesses that are accessing the same services. All you need is to be able to access QuickBooks online. Some of the benefits that business people get to enjoy from this are:

1. Time savings: time is an important element in any business. Saving time might result to better results in a business since more time is sent on things that matter more in the business for the realization of better results. Cloud computing is one way through which a business can save a considerable amount of time. This is because technology and data are always available and you can count on them. One thing business people should know about is that with cloud computing, you will not have to manage your software and you will also not have to go back and forth to visit your clients or even to spend plenty of time on data entry. This is what will save you ample time as well as your business and also your clients

2. Cloud computing gives you anytime, anywhere access: the functionality of cloud is accessible to you anywhere you will be at any given time. You can access your work at any time of day or night, from wherever you might be across the globe. You always get an always-on connection to your client's data, therefore you can still

serve your clients from wherever you might be. You also do not have to deal with time zone restrictions whenever you are filing your tax returns. This means that you are free to do so much from anywhere, anytime, for instance:

- Adding and editing employees, customers or vendors

- Viewing reports pertaining to balance sheet and profit & loss

- Creating and emailing invoices

- Viewing balances from your Bank account and credit card

- Accessing the lists of your vendors, customers, and employee

- Access of information pertaining to your debtors and creditors

3. Cloud computing makes it easy for you to work with your clients: this is one program that will intensify the bond you have with your clients, without any costs. If you have clients who want to be involved in any business operation, you will find this program really helpful. Your clients can see what work is in progress, how much has been accomplished and what still needs to be done. This is what keeps an open communication between your clients and the business.

4. It is easy to afford. With cloud computing, you can be sure that you will afford all the benefits that it comes with. To start with, there are no license fees and this

means that the initial costs are already taken care of. Generally speaking, you will incur less costs, which is good for business.

Chapter 4:
QuickBooks Tips and Tricks

Any business finance software is supposed to make accounting much easier and more reliable and QuickBooks is a very easy to use software. However, there is always a way that you can make things easier even when you are using this software. This will make achieving your desired results easier than you previously thought. If you have already started QuickBooks, here are some tips and tricks that can help you achieve more from QuickBooks:

1. Use of keyboard shortcuts: most if not all windows-based applications come with some shortcuts that can make working easy for you and QuickBooks is not exceptional. There are several shortcuts that you can always employ in order to work faster and to enjoy your accounting, some of these are:

   ✓ Ctrl-I to create an invoice

   ✓ Ctrl-N to open a new items like a check, invoice, a bill

   ✓ Ctrl-F to find a transaction

   ✓ Ctrl-W to write a new check

   ✓ Ctrl-E to edit a transaction that has been selected in the register

   ✓ Ctrl-J to open customer support center

   ✓ Ctrl-M to memorize a certain transaction or report

2. Customizing the icon bar to suit your needs: a new QuickBooks program will come with a default icons bar at the top of the screen. This bar can be customized in order to suit your preference and needs. This can be done by removing, adding or even modifying some icons to ensure that they fit just what you need to work with. Removing an item form the icons bar for instance can be achieved by clicking on it and hitting the delete button. To add an icon on the other hand, you will click on the field where you want to add the icon, click on item, hit the add button then select the icons that you want to add from the drop down menu. You can also change the way icons appear on the icon bar or even add separators, just what you want for your icons bar.

3. Right click on menus anywhere in the program: doing this will be much easier than going for the icons and menus on the tool bar. If you want to do something on the menu, you can right click on it and do whatever needs to be done. If for instance you want to make changes on a certain entry in the Chart of counts, you can right click on it and then you will be able to delete it, edit it, customize it or anything that you prefer. This makes changing anything much easier and faster.

4. Use of the QuickMath calculator: QuickBooks comes with its own calculator. To access it, you click on 'edit' then 'use calculator'. However, the QuickMath calculator will be much easier and better to use. To use it, click on the field where you want to make a calculation, click on the = sign to get a mini-tape. Type in the numbers that will be used in the calculation followed by the sign that you want to use in the calculation. If you want to clear out an entry, click once on C but to clear everything from the tape, you will have

to click on C twice. To cancel the entry calculation, click on Esc

5. Use of Classes to track profit and loss better: elements of a business are categorized in classes in QuickBooks. Every entry that you enter will be categorized under a certain class. Class reports are important because they are the ones that determine if the business is getting into a loss or making profits. Whenever you are working with your reference, you have to make sure that classes are turned on. This way, every transaction that you enter will be categorized under a certain class. With this, you should be able to get a class report of every element in your business to know how well or ad you are doing.

6. Backing your data up to the cloud: the program will come with a wizard that will take you through the process of backing up your data up to the cloud. This ensures that your data will be absolutely safe and that it can be accessible from any computer anywhere, anytime. This comes at a small cost though, but the benefits you get here are more than what you pay for them.

7. Use of edit/preferences feature: a QuickBooks program will come with a set up wizard that will help you set up the groundwork for your business. You do not have to stick to this wizard though because it is not comprehensive. You can edit to the kind of setup that you want for your business, one that suits your business needs. To do this, you will have to click on the edit/preferences button to make more decisions, which are not available in the setup wizard. Some of the decisions that you can make here are for instance the

kind of default accounts you will be using for writing checks and paying bills, the default annual interest rate you will be using for your business, if you want to create estimates or not, whether or not you want to use payroll, the kinds of reminders you will be using among others.

8. If you are using more than one checking account in your business, you can always change the background color of your accounts in order to easily identify one account from the other/others. To do this, open the register for any of the checking accounts whose background color you want to change, click on the edit menu then select 'change account color'. This will make it easy for you to identify one account from the others.

Chapter 5:
QuickBooks for Inventory

Businesses which deal with items for sale, whether small or large, needs to keep track of their inventory. This is what makes it easy for you to avail what your customers need at any given time without fail. With proper inventory, serving your customers effectively and on time all the time is made easy and this is what gains your business a good reputation. Besides, you are able to keep a good track record of what you have sold and what you still have in stock, which is important in balancing of accounts and helping you with payment of taxes. With such records, you will easily know when to place more order for more goods so that you will not run out of stock, which can inconvenience your clients. This can be hard to do if you are doing it manually but with QuickBooks, it can be done in no time and more accurately.

Setting up QuickBooks inventory

QuickBooks inventory is usually more involved and it can be harder when compared to other areas in the business. This is maybe because inventory affects all the other areas in a business, starting with sales, purchasing, production, accounting, shipping among others. This is the entry that shows workflow processes in a business, because the transaction that one person handles in a given department will result to another transaction in the same or different department

Another reason why this is the most important entry is because so many lists come into play once inventory is affected and the entire database is affected in the end. What this means is that once a transaction has been executed, vendor and customer information in the database is touched. Every item in the inventory has so many attributes, for instance the average cost, the selling price, buying price, unit of measure among so many others. Again, the item has to go through several transactional processes. If an item is being bought for instance, it will have to go through the purchase orders, item receipts, and vendor bills among others. If it is being sold, there are such transaction processes like sales orders, estimates, packing lists, pick tickets, invoices among others. In short, transactions under inventory are connected to so many other entries that are affected once a single transaction is made, that is why this is the most complex thing you will handle with QuickBooks.

Many people make the mistake of rushing through inventory just as they would do when handling a simple data entry then they realize the mistake they have made when it is already too late. You need to adopt a systematic approach in order to set up your inventory in an accurate manner:

Prepare your lists

Your inventory is not just about the list of items; there are other lists that you have to prepare for instance the chart of accounts, the units of measure, the vendor lists, the location and tracking lists among others. Your lists will form the foundation for the inventory. The good thing about using QuickBooks here is that all the items will be connected to the financial accounts, therefore you will not have to worry so much about the accounting bit because it is already taken care of. What you do is that you start with the accounting part, then connect all the items you will enter in the inventory to the account one at a time. You will not have to go back to balance your accounts when this is done the right way.

First of all let us consider the main accounts in the Chart of Accounts, which affect any items in the inventory:

- An Inventory Asset account that is on the Balance Sheet

- An Income account that is on the Profit & Loss Statement or income statement

- A Cost of Goods Sold account which is also on the Profit & Loss Statement.

You have to choose which of these three accounts you will attach to your items, the ones which will help you make the best reports and accurate financial results. To do this, turn on the inventory function in QuickBooks by the administrator, go to Edit, then Preferences, Items and Inventory, Company Preferences tab then click to activate Inventory and purchase orders. When this is done, your software will automatically create an Inventory Asset account as the other asset type of account, which cannot be changed again.

You might need to create other Inventor Asset accounts depending on how the company plans to trail the value of their inventory. If for instance you are a manufacturing company that needs to track the work-in-progress, you might need several of these accounts but for a distributor, one account will be enough.

Pay attention to the Inventory valuation summary report, which lists down everything in the inventory and all the items in the stock lists. This is the report which shows balances in the inventory asset accounts. The total in this report and the totals in the inventory asset account can be used as a checks and balances to show that you are recording your items properly, therefore both of them should always match.

The next bit you should take care of is the creation of a **Sales or Income account**. This is the second most important account type in the Charts of Accounts. A mistake that is common with many QuickBooks beginners is that they create so many income accounts probably for every product that they deal with. These many accounts will be hard to manage in the end and you will be spending so much time on it, more than you should. An easier way out is to have maybe two or three accounts for your product lines. If you want to track down profitability for instance, you can easily do this through reports=Jobs, Time and Mileage=Item Profitability Report. It is important to know that items in your business will all get connected to one account, therefore if you are selling to different people and you want to track down your sales separately, it is easier to use classes in QuickBooks than to create different accounts for them.

The third most important account under Charts of Accounts is the **Cost of Goods Sold account**. This account is automatically created once you turn on the inventory function in QuickBooks. With this account too, there might be need for more than one account, although it is not really necessary unless there is a good reason for it. It is important to know that every item you will have in your inventory will only connect to one of these accounts therefore only create an additional account if you have a need for additional reports.

After the accounts have been created, you can now work on the **Units of Measure**. This is the trickiest lists under inventory in QuickBooks. This list will determine the kind of goods you will receive, the kind of stock you will keep and also the kinds of goods you will be selling. You will have to decide if you will be dealing with multiple units of measure or just a single unit, which is bought and sold on the same unit. This function will be turned on under the Preferences=Items and Inventory. Before you set your Units of Measure list, consider these issues:

- The base unit of items- this will be the smallest unit of items that have been received, stacked or sold. This is the unit that will be used to determine the unit which will be used in purchases and sales, because these units come as multiples of the base unit. This way, you will not have to deal with fractions or another unit.

- The base unit will be the only one that will reflect in QuickBooks' Inventory Stock Status report. You will not get any report pertaining to multiple units in your stocks.

- Different types of units of measure can be set up for instance weight, volume etc but ensure that the quantities of these units will not change depending on the product that has been affected.

The **vendor list** is another important list you will have to consider before you start recording items in your inventory. You can have this list compiled then import it into the QuickBooks file like many business people do. Ensure that you have an up-to-date vendor list so as to save time since you will not have to specify the vendor later on.

If you are using an advanced inventory function, you will have two more lists to prepare: location list and also serial or lot number tracking list. You can prepare the location ahead of time, then add it to the inventory function through the Lists dropdown menu.

Types of items in the items list

Now that you have all the lists prepared, you can now proceed to the list of items. Here are the basic types of items that you will have under this list:

1. Services: under this category, you will record the labor that is purchased from a vendor or labor that has been included in an invoice for a customer. If it is just used for your customers, it will only need to connect to an income account.

2. The inventory: this will have a list of raw materials or items that are needed for resale and this part will help in case you want to trail the quantity that is in stock. The value of items in this list will be under inventory asset account until they are sold, because this is the time their cost will be recognized through their invoice.

3. Non-inventory parts: these are items that are only expensed at the time of purchase. With this items, the manager does not really know how many they are at any given time. These items will appear in the purchase and sale documents.

4. Inventory assemblies: this is a list of items that are as a result of assembling of components or items that have been produced through raw materials processing/manufacturing. Again, the value of items here will be stored in the inventory asset account until the items are sold, which is when their costs will be recognized through the invoice.

5. Group Items: these are items in components that are sold as just one item. Once they are sold, that is the time QuickBooks will reduce the quantity of their

components. These items are usually not kept in stock therefore their quantities are not usually tracked.

6. The other charge: these may not be actual inventory items but they are related to inventory although it is hard to specify a unit of measure on them. These are for instance handling charges.

7. there are so many other items types you might want to include for instance discounts, sales tax, payments among other although they do not affect inventory directly.

It is important to determine the inventory type where your items will fall into first, then you can easily enter them in those categories. The inventories list and the assemblies for instance will connect to the three accounts I mentioned above while services, other charge and non-inventory items can use the purchasing account, the sales account or both of them, depending on whether the items has been sold or bought or it has been bought for resale. Group item on the other hand will not be connected to any of these accounts because their existence is after a certain component has been removed.

Chapter 6:
Mistakes to Avoid

The way that you keep your company's files talks a lot about the kind of person you are and the kind of business that you are running. So many business people strive to keep their business record in good order but most of them do not success and the funny bit is that most of the mistakes that they make are similar. Sometimes making such mistakes happens even when you are very careful that is why it is important to know some of these common mistake so that you will be careful with in order to leave all your financial statements accurate and easy to interpret.

1. Failing to reconcile your accounts: accounts recociliaution is very important because the integrity of any account is dependent on reconciliation. Reconciliations ensure that what you have in all your accounts is correct, that is why it is a very important part of the process. Do not just concentrate on your checking and savings accounts but also on liabilities, which include loans and taxes. Also ensure that you check on asset accounts as well, since all the accounts are important in any business. This is the only way you will be sure that everything in your register is accurate.

2. Skipping credit card accounts: many business people will not include their credit card into the QuickBooks, which is a regrettable mistake. This issue of creating an expense account every time you credit your credit card, or making it an item in the check window is not good. You need to have an account for that, just like a checking account so that you will keep your records well and easy to follow through. Once you make a payment

into the credit card, it should be a transfer of money to the credit card and nothing else.

3. Deleting transactions: there is no single transaction in QuickBooks that work independently; all of them are connected to other transactions, therefore any change that you will make on one transaction will affect so many others. If you delete one entry for instance, you will change the entire data. You need to check with your accountant first before deleting any transaction to ensure that it is not affecting many entries in your system.

4. Failing to review the balance sheet: reviewing your balance sheet will help you understand the financial health of your business. Since the balance sheet reflects all the accounts you have in your business. It is easy to know how well you are doing, or even how bad things are. Your statements from the accounts should all match, otherwise you should know that there is a major issue in your business. This is the only way you can make sound decisions pertaining to your business in order to better its performance.

5. Not using your purchase order system: this is a very important tool but not many people get to enjoy its usefulness. What you do is to make sure that you create a purchase order very time you make an order from a vendor. You always have to ensure that you are receiving your orders against that PO. Do not keep such records for over a year though so as not to keep records that are no longer useful in your system.

6. Use of multiple accounts and subaccounts: this is what creates a messy chart of accounts and it is a mistake

that many bookkeepers make because they think that it will help them understand the reports better. However, this will take so much of your time and your reports can be confusing for another person who will be reading them. You do not need so many subaccounts when you can group some of these items together into one account. Instead of having separate accounts for pen and papers for instance, you can have a stationary account for them all. Keep your accounts as simple as possible.

7. A disorderly items list: every product that you sell will be listed as items in QuickBooks. Sometimes people just record and inventory anywhere and they do not remember to keep the records updated. You need to clean this up because it will mess up your entire records. In order to achieve a clean items list, deactivate all the items that you are no longer selling. All the items should fall under inventory and non-inventory categories. Also, ensure that the costs for each items is up to date. You should also double check the items that are in stock at all times.

8. Use of incorrect report settings: report settings are very important, hence you have to ensure that you are using them in their correct settings. This way, you will get the proper report when you need it. Accrual reports for instance should give you information pertaining to the overall performance of your business. Cash reports on the other hand should show you how cash is flowing in and out of the business.

Conclusion

Success in a business is dependent on a lot of things and organization is one of them. An organized business has higher chances of success than a poorly ordered business. This explains why so many small businesses are relying on QuickBooks in order to warrant that all their financial records are up to date and easy to understand.

One of the benefits that you will get from this is increase in productivity. QuickBooks will help you come into terms with the performance of your business, therefore you are able to make sound decisions based on he reports that you are receiving. This way, you can act quickly to get better results faster, and by the end of the year, your production will be much better than it previously was. It is very easy for a business person to reach its full potential once he starts bookkeeping, because he can now spend wisely, knowing that too much expenditure is affecting the income of the business. This is important for your investors too, and they can willingly invest for the growth of the business because everything is clear to them.

QuickBooks are slowly gaining fame, with the latest QuickBooks 2016 program offering better features and more chances for small businesses to do much better. It is the desire of everyone in business to reap something great from their business and this is one tool of operation that can guarantee that. That is why learning QuickBooks is good idea for everyone in a business setting.

www.ingramcontent.com/pod-product-compliance
Lightning Source LLC
Chambersburg PA
CBHW070304190526
45169CB00004B/1523